Developing a Generation of Conviction

Men of Honor and Women of Worth

Julie Spier

CLAY BRIDGES
PRESS

Developing a Generation of Conviction
Men of Honor and Women of Worth

ISBN 978-1-953300-47-8 (paperback)
ISBN 978-1-953300-48-5 (ebook)

Special Sales: Most Clay Bridges titles are available in special quantity discounts. Custom imprinting or excerpting can also be done to fit special needs. For standard bulk orders, go to www.claybridgesbulk.com. For specialty press or large orders, contact Clay Bridges at info@claybridgespress.com.

*This curriculum is dedicated to my husband, Dave,
a true man of honor, and to my little world-changers
Owen, Maddox, and Sophie. It is also dedicated
to my parents, who empowered my heart to do Kingdom
work and instilled in me a drive for integrity.*

CONTENTS

ABOUT THIS CURRICULUM

Romans 12:1–2 calls us to not conform to the patterns of this world. But every day, lies from our culture and traps from Satan entice young people who love the Lord into making decisions that look no different from those of their non-Christian peers. Christians must filter through lots of messages from our culture that either blatantly or deceptively tell them what is valued for their gender even as masculinity and femininity are defined in ways that completely contradict Scripture. We need to develop young men of honor and young women of worth.

This curriculum is unique in that it will ask men and women to study their own gender as well as the opposite gender. This approach will help each person define what it means to be a godly man or woman and empower them to treat each other with respect.

LESSON 1

Say What?:

Living Radically Different from Our Culture

Introduction

Romans 12:1–2 calls Christ-followers to live set apart from their culture. How does our culture define masculinity? How does our culture define femininity?

Bible Study

• What does being a man of God look like?

Read:

- Proverbs 10:9 (integrity)

- Ephesians 5:25 (sacrificial and loving husband)

- Ephesians 6:4 (disciplined and purposeful parenting)

- Romans 12:10 (humble)

- Proverbs 27:17 (accountable)

- Philippians 4:8 (pure and honorable)

- Titus 2:2 (self-controlled, sound in faith)

• What does being a woman of God look like?

- Proverbs 31 (virtuous, hardworking, wise, caring)

- Ephesians 5:22 (God-fearing, respectful wife)

- Titus 2:3–5 (pure, devoted mother; kind)

- 1 Peter 3:3–4 (gentle spirit, modest)

• What rewards do you receive for living to fit into our culture?

• What rewards do you receive for living to honor God?

• Which reward from our culture is most tempting to you? Why?

• In what ways do you blend into our culture too much? What needs to change so you are living to honor God more?

Many of us want to live for God, but we have to figure out how to do so in a culture of lust, materialism, selfishness, and pride. The difference between what our culture celebrates and what God desires is obvious—we must choose who we're going to please. Living wrapped up in our culture is destructive if we decide that we desire to please God. This is why Scripture gives strong commands about how to deal with sin.

Read:

- Ephesians 6:11

- Mark 9:43–47

- Ephesians 5:3

- Proverbs 14:16

- Psalm 119:11

• Why are we sometimes lazy when dealing with sin?

• What sins are a struggle for you?

• What is your typical attitude when it comes to dealing with sin? What steps can you take to improve that attitude?

To live a life that honors God, we must become completely dissatisfied with the life our culture tries to entice us to live. We must see that living a hypocritical or half-hearted life for the Lord is detestable to Him.

Read and discuss Revelation 3:15–16.

In the coming lessons, we'll dive more into what it looks like to become a man of honor and a woman of worth. For now, understand that it's a calling to live radically different from our culture. If we develop a generation of men of honor and women of worth, we might see changes in statistics about eating disorders, anger, pornography, depression, jealousy, and divorce—to name a few.

Too often, we become plagued with shame and guilt as we attempt to become better disciples of Christ. We need to surrender to God and let Him be the one who changes us and empowers fruit in our lives. We need to believe and determine to be men of honor and women of worth and then devote ourselves to God so He can make it happen within us.

Challenge

- Read God's Word for 15 minutes a day.

- Spend time every day in prayer asking God to mold your attitude and character.

Notes

_____

_____

_____

_____

_____

_____

_____

_____

_____

_____

Notes

_____

_____

_____

_____

_____

_____

_____

_____

_____

_____

_____

Notes

_____

_____

_____

_____

_____

_____

_____

_____

_____

_____

_____

Lesson 2

Sweatpants and Ice Cream:

Affirming the Women God Created Us to Be

Women's Study—Introduction

Have you ever had those days when you just want to stay in sweats all day and gorge yourself on chocolate ice cream? If so, chances are it was boy drama, friendship problems, or self-esteem issues that brought you to such a low point. Unfortunately, we live in a pretty critical world, and it can be difficult to maintain any sort of positive self-esteem. It's tragic how our culture's emphasis on physical beauty, popularity, and materialism confuses, beats down, and distracts women from remembering what God finds beautiful and valuable.

Would you believe me if I told you that larger, curvier women may be considered more attractive than skinny women? In some cultures, a larger, fuller bottom is considered to be a woman's most attractive feature, but this is not necessarily true in the United States. What is it that determines what we find beautiful? Our culture displays what's valued through the media; women are constantly bombarded with messages about what makes them beautiful from movies, social media, and advertisements. US media portrays an "ideal" female body that less than 5 percent of women can attain, according to research findings on body image reported by Kate Fox in "Mirror, Mirror."[1] Consequently, women are left to feel insecure, ugly, and angry. The struggle within for positive self-esteem can be a huge dilemma for Christian women. We know that we should be happy with who God made us to be, and yet every day, we're measured by the standards of our culture, and we feel like we don't measure up.

Satan can easily trap women in the mindset of feeling unappreciated and insecure. The next thing we know, we're physically engaging with men in ways we know we shouldn't because we need to feel loved, or we're treating our friends poorly because of jealousy. It's easy to become exhausted by feelings of insecurity, guilt, and inadequacy—I know; I have experienced such feelings.

Are you willing to explore how to become a woman of worth—a woman who finds her value in the Lord? Doing so changes everything. Let's build a foundation for Christian women to stand firm on.

Romans 12:2 tells Christ-followers not to conform to their culture. Could we start by admitting that our culture is biased, judgmental, and misguided? Women need to identify messages from our culture as negative and detrimental and not allow Satan to convince them to be caught up in them.

Too often, we feel insignificant if we don't see ourselves as physically attractive, and this outlook taints our ability to focus on qualities such as honesty, humility, compassion, and grace. Maybe you're not sure you have the strength to be a woman of worth; let's just start at the beginning.

If you are open and willing, God can fill you with the peace and joy that will allow you to be confident in yourself and affirming toward others. This will bring you greater satisfaction than fitting into our culture ever could!

Men's Study – Introduction

You must be thinking, "Why in the world are we going to talk about girl stuff?" I know it might seem weird, but this is very intentional. As young men, you need to understand the lies from our culture that negatively affect women so you can play a role in encouraging and leading them. Learning what women deal with and how to help them stay focused on God is a way for you to honor your mom, sister, female friend, future wife, and future children.

Our culture so emphasizes physical beauty, popularity, and materialism that it's easy for Christian women to become confused, beaten down, and distracted instead of remembering what God finds beautiful and valuable.

What if I told your sister that larger, curvier women may be considered more attractive than skinny women? She wouldn't believe me. Why not? In some cultures, a larger, fuller bottom is considered to be a woman's most attractive feature—but this is not true in the United States. What is it that determines what we find beautiful? Our culture displays what's valued through the media; women are constantly bombarded with messages about what makes them beautiful from movies, social media, and advertisements. US media portrays an "ideal" female body that less than 5 percent of women can attain, according to research findings reported by Kate Fox in "Mirror, Mirror."[2]

Women are left to feel insecure, ugly, and angry. For Christian women, the struggle within for positive self-esteem can be a huge dilemma. They know that they should be happy with who God made them to be, and yet every day, they are measured by the standards of our culture and feel like they don't measure up.

Satan can easily trap them in the mindset of feeling unappreciated and insecure. This can lead women to physically engage with men in ways they know they shouldn't because they need to feel loved or to treat their friends poorly because of jealousy. They become exhausted by feelings of insecurity, guilt, and inadequacy. A woman of worth finds her value in the Lord, and that changes everything. You can be hugely helpful in giving women a firm foundation to stand on when you see them and value them as God does.

Romans 12:2 tells Christ-followers not to conform to their culture. Could we start by admitting that our culture is biased, judgmental, and misguided? Women feel insignificant if they don't have sex appeal, and that taints their ability to focus on qualities such as honesty, humility, compassion, and grace. As a young man, you can help the women in your life feel worth regardless of their physical beauty. This will go a long way in helping them not get caught up in the lies of Satan.

Women's Study

In *The Search for Significance*, author Robert McGee says that people fall into various traps, which include trying to meet certain standards and be approved by certain people so they can feel good about themselves.[3]

- What traps do women usually fall into?

- What standards do women try to meet?

- Who do women feel the need to receive approval from?

- Make a list of the top issues that women deal with regarding their identity. By what criteria are they most judged?

Women feel a great deal of pressure to be beautiful, so physical beauty was likely included in all your lists. Author Ginny Olson reports the following findings on this topic:

> In a study of 548 middle school and high school girls, 59% reported that they were displeased with their bodies. Our media projects a Barbie-like body as the ideal, but the probability of having a body with the same proportions is 1 in 100,000.[4]

- How important is physical beauty? How much does it affect a woman's self-esteem? Why?

- How does the desire for physical beauty affect women?

Low self-esteem can lead women to engage in unhealthy eating habits, self-harm, poor choices with men, immodesty, jealousy, depression, and other issues.

- What lowers your self-esteem? Why?

- What poor choices have you made because you were trying to please someone other than God?

Read Psalm 139. God knit each of us together with a plan and a purpose. When we find a way to affirm who God made us to be, we can silence Satan and our culture.

- Do you believe it's possible for you to have positive self-esteem? Why or why not?

- How can you improve your self-esteem?

- How can you be purposeful to avoid some of the pitfalls that women fall into due to low self-esteem?

Challenge

- Read Psalm 139 every day this week.

- Identify the lies you usually believe and find truths from God's Word to counter them. Write down those truths and put them somewhere very visible to you.

Men's Study

At summer camp one year, students participated in a team-building activity that involved carrying a team member for a short distance. At one point during the activity, a male student picked up a female student and slipped, which caused him to drop her a little bit. To hide his embarrassment, he sarcastically yelled, "Wow, you're heavier than I expected!" The young woman laughed it off, and the exercise came to a close. Later that night, a youth leader found that young woman in the bathroom making herself throw up. "I'm fat and ugly," she said with tears in her eyes. That young man didn't understand that this young woman had struggled for years with an eating disorder and that his one negative comment would have such an effect.

- What did you learn from this lesson about what women deal with? Did anything surprise you?

- What specific things can you do to build worth into women?

- What specific behavior can you change to avoid causing women to feel insecure?

- What do you need to change in terms of how you interact with the women in your life?

Challenge

- Do something or say something every day this week to build worth into a woman in your life.

Notes

_____

_____

_____

_____

_____

_____

_____

_____

_____

_____

Notes

LESSON 3

Developing a Sisterhood:

Relying on God's Spirit to Remove Insecurity and Jealousy

Introduction

Let's be honest: There's some truth to the term *mean girls*. Women can be manipulative, catty, and gossipy. Jealousy and insecurity can cause women to deceive and exclude one another. Too often, women's insecurities, fears, and selfish motives are the reasons behind what they do, how they treat people, and the way in which they dress.

As we discussed in the previous lesson, finding worth in the Lord is key for women. If they can learn to affirm who God made them to be, they can also become more selfless and able to affirm others. Christian women need to build each other up, not tear each other down. This will set a radical example of the power of Christ to non-Christian women.

Women's Study

- Choose your top three words to describe how women tend to behave toward one another. Why do you think they act this way?

- Do you struggle with insecurity? In what ways?

- Do you struggle with jealousy? How do you display it?

- How difficult is it to not participate in gossip?

- How can women change the way they treat each other?

Read:

    ▫ Colossians 3:12–14

    ▫ 2 Timothy 1:7

God promises us a spirit of self-control, meaning we're not powerless to our jealous insecurities—we can choose to keep them in check and encourage others. A woman confident in the Lord is able to appreciate the gifts of others and celebrate their successes because she's relying on God's Spirit to remove jealousy and insecurity from her heart.

- How can you personally be more affirming?

Spend time together in prayer asking God to convict you when your attitude is selfish. Ask for His help in being humble, caring, selfless, appreciative, and encouraging.

Challenge

- Any time you identify something about another woman that you admire, tell her. Celebrate her successes and gifts.

- Do **not** participate in any gossip or catty behavior.

Men's Study

- What frustrates you about the way women act or treat each other? Why?

- What do you think are the main motivations behind their actions?

- What role do you think men play?

Women tend to be much more emotional about things than men. They also dwell on and analyze things to death. For example, if a man shows up at a meeting and recognizes that his friends didn't save him a seat, it's not a big deal. If anything, he might lightly punch his friends and say something sarcastic like, "See if I save you a seat from now on." He'll find somewhere else to sit and then let it drop. However, if a woman shows up and recognizes that her friends didn't save her a seat, she's likely to be upset. She'll wonder whether they're mad at her or whether they want to sit with someone else rather than her. The seat snafu will cause her to feel insecure, angry, jealous, and lonely. When women feel this way, they often talk about it with other women, which can turn into gossip and "drama."

- Do you understand the difference between how men interact and how women interact? What are the main differences you've noticed?

- How do you think men can help women interact better?

Many times, men will blow off women's behavior, saying things like, "You're just being overdramatic" or "It's not a big a deal." Instead, men could choose to listen, provide truthful, gentle encouragement, and pray. What a powerful difference! Don't be fooled; all women struggle with insecurities—some just hide it better than others. All women can use an encouraging word or action from the men in their lives.

Read Colossians 3:12–14.

Spend time in prayer for the women in your life.

Challenge

• Commit to pray on behalf of your mom, sister, female friend, future wife, and future children.

Notes

_____

_____

_____

_____

_____

_____

_____

_____

_____

_____

_____

Notes

_____

_____

_____

_____

_____

_____

_____

_____

_____

_____

_____

Notes

LESSON 4

The Power of Respect:

Developing Wives Who "Get It"

Introduction

It's pretty obvious that men and women are different. They think differently, approach problems differently, communicate differently, and so on. Men and women can both be well-intentioned, but because they're different, it can be difficult to see each other's intentions as good. It's important that we understand one another if we're going to be able to encourage the opposite gender.

• What are the main ways that men and women are different?

God demonstrates that men and women are different through how He directs them in Scripture—specifically in Ephesians. When we look at Ephesians, we see the writer use very specific words to describe how women should treat men: "Each one of you also must love his wife as he loves himself, and the wife must respect her husband" (Eph. 5:33).

Women's Study

- What do you think of when you hear the word *respect*? Why?

- How do you think positive self-esteem plays into how you treat men?

Perhaps God asks women to be respectful of men because He uniquely designed men to need respect to feel loved. Men desire to feel valued, supported, and trusted, which God commands women to do in Ephesians. The problem is that society has warped us into equating respect with inferiority.

Typically, what happens is that instead of meeting men's greatest need, women act defensive, prideful, and selfish. Here's the thing, though—the verses in Ephesians Chapter

5 call us to respect our husbands as we would Christ. In other words, we have no excuse! Now, I know that many of you might be thinking: "Uh, I'm not married!" But these verses contain applicable truths for us before we are married. God is teaching us how to treat the opposite gender, and we can practice now to honor men in our lives and to prepare for our future spouse. When we are willing to respect men, they are empowered; realize the great influence you have and be intentional to build up the men in your life.

Oftentimes, women won't respect men because they feel like the man doesn't deserve it. Without respect, men feel deflated and unmotivated, which makes them act in ways that cause women to disrespect them even more.

- What are some disrespectful things that women do toward men?

- Is respect earned? Should a woman only respect a man if he deserves it?

- What are some tangible ways that you can serve, respect, and support the men in your life?

Challenge

- Don't poke fun at men, but rather appreciate their efforts and speak encouragement.

Men's Study

- What do you guess women think of when they hear the word *respect*?

- What ways do some men lead or act that make women wary of respecting them?

- Is respect earned? Should a woman respect a man even if he doesn't deserve it?

- What makes you respect another man?

Oftentimes, women won't respect men because they feel like men don't deserve it. Without respect, men feel deflated and unmotivated, which makes them act in ways that cause women to disrespect them even more. This is an unhealthy cycle; women are being challenged to respect you so as to empower you. Talk for a few minutes about what you think men can do to ensure respect and to maintain integrity.

- What qualities gain respect?

- How should you handle it if you are feeling disrespected or deflated?

- What does it mean to be a respectable, godly man?

Close in prayer.

Challenge

- Be disciplined to ensure you are full of integrity.

- Don't shut down; if you feel disrespected or deflated, be purposeful in communicating to resolve the issue.

Notes

_____

_____

_____

_____

_____

_____

_____

_____

_____

_____

Notes

_____

_____

_____

_____

_____

_____

_____

_____

_____

_____

_____

Notes

_____

_____

_____

_____

_____

_____

_____

_____

_____

_____

_____

Lesson 5

It's Just the Right Thing:

Striving to Be Men of Character

Men's Study – Introduction

Our culture tells men to be macho, self-sufficient machines that show no emotion. Many men, however, are full of a variety of emotions that they don't know how to deal with. Deep down, Christian men want to live for God, but they feel beaten down and ashamed. Because Satan attacks when we're feeling weak and isolated, trying to deal with these big feelings on our own allows sin to prevail.

In Romans 7:15, Paul said, "I do not understand what I do. For what I want to do I do not do, but what I hate I do." God forgave and utilized Paul, and He can do the same for us. The first step is turning to God with genuine brokenness and repentance, allowing Him to show us grace. God has all the strength to help men surrender emotions such as anger, lust, and pride to become men full of integrity, compassion, purity, and humility. This type of man gains the respect of others because of his character—he's the kind of man girls dream about marrying.

Our culture would love for men to believe that their lives should be all about earning money, being successful, and having pleasurable experiences. Sure, it might be fun for men to feed their ego and do what brings them pleasure for a while, but those choices don't go without consequences. For example, a man might have to break his wife's heart one day when he tells her about all the sexual sin he committed with his various girlfriends in high school. There are consequences for a man's relationship with God, too. As a man makes choices that please himself rather than God, he'll fall farther and farther away from God. He'll make excuses and justify his behavior, but he'll be filled with regret when he tries to turn back to God. Every man should ask himself, "What kind of man do I want to be?" I'm not talking about in 20 years—I'm talking about right now. Every day, choices flesh out the future.

People find the male characters in movies like *Braveheart* compelling because they're willing to fight for what they believe in. They show conviction over injustices and choose to do something about them. Think about men from the Bible like Daniel; we admire Daniel for his bravery to stand up for his faith. This is the kind of man that Christian men are called to be. Our culture makes it appealing to live a selfish life of pleasure and materialism, but Christian men are called to something much greater. Christian men shouldn't settle; they shouldn't succumb to the petty accolades this world will give them on the surface. They should stand up for what they believe in: justice, grace, and respect.

God created men with a desire to be heroic, to serve, and to protect. Imagine if Christian men could flesh out the great natural tendencies God designed within them to build up others, live with conviction and integrity, and change their communities. Christian men need to decide right now how masculinity is correctly defined. Which paints the best picture of masculinity: our culture or Scripture? If they decide to live according to Scripture, Christian men will have to accept that our culture may define them as weak, insignificant, and possibly even feminine.

- What are the most difficult cultural expectations for you to deal with? Why?

- What sinful traps do you fall into?

Women's Study – Introduction

Our culture tells men to be macho, self-sufficient machines that show no emotions. They're supposed to always be strong, independent, and successful, while also showing a sensitive and romantic side. Many Christian men are full of a variety of emotions that they don't know how to deal with. Deep down, they want to live for God, but they become ashamed and feel beaten down. Oftentimes, men try to deal with things on their own, which can allow sin to prevail, worsening their shame.

In Romans 7:15, Paul said, "I do not understand what I do. For what I want to do I do not do, but what I hate I do." God forgave and utilized Paul, and He can do the same for the men in your life. Their first step is turning to

God with genuine brokenness and repentance, allowing Him to show grace. God has all the strength to help men surrender emotions such as anger, lust, and pride to become men of compassion, purity, and humility. We can help by providing them with understanding and support—not condemnation or teasing. Think about the kind of man you want to marry; you can help encourage the men in your life toward becoming that kind of man.

Our culture would love for men to believe that their lives should be all about earning money, being successful, and having pleasurable experiences. It's easy for men to believe that it's fun to feed their ego or pursue pleasure, but those choices don't go without consequences. Their choices have consequences for their relationship with God as well as their future life and relationships. The more a man falls into sin, the more excuses he'll make to justify his behavior, perpetuating regret and shame. Young men need to consider what kind of men they want to be. I'm not talking about in 20 years—I'm talking about right now. Their choices flesh that out.

People find the male characters in movies like *Braveheart* compelling because they're willing to fight for what they believe in. They show conviction over injustices and choose to do something about them. Think about men from the Bible like Daniel; we admire Daniel for his bravery to stand up for his faith because that defines him as a man of honor. Our culture makes it appealing to live a selfish life of pleasure and materialism, but God calls men to something much greater. As women, we can help men not to settle for the petty accolades this world will give them on the surface. They need to stand up for what they believe in: justice, grace, and respect.

General Discussion

- What are the greatest differences between what God desires in a man and what our culture says is masculine?

- What pressures do men deal with every day? How are they told to deal with these pressures? What consequences can come from their actions?

In *Teenage Guys: Exploring Issues Adolescent Guys Face and Strategies to Help Them*, author Steve Gerali lists what young men need. His list includes the following needs:[5]

- *Men need to be known and understood.*

  It can be hard for men to be vulnerable, but it's worth the time and effort because they need to feel valued for who they really are.

- *Men need validation and empowerment as unique individuals.*

  According to Gerali, we need to realize that a universal label can make a man feel as though he isn't a man or that he cannot become one. To make one issue "every guy's battle" or journey or need robs him of his uniqueness. We need to help guys discover their unique talents, skills, abilities, characteristics, flaws, needs, and weaknesses.

- *Men need community and mentors.*

  Gerali observes that men are clan oriented. Within their community, they need the closeness of other men who act as a compass for their manhood.

- *Men need to work and to play.*

  Hard work builds responsibility and can be an act of worship to God. Men also have a natural drive to play or seek adventure; it can teach them about character, discipline, teamwork, and much more.

- Discuss this list of needs.

- Do you agree with these needs? Are there any needs that you would add or omit?

Men's Study

- Considering the list above, which ones are most true for you?

- How can we be sure these needs are being met for one another?

Pray for one another.

Challenge

- Surrender culture's definition of masculinity and commit to a biblical definition of masculinity.

- Read about Daniel's life (Dan. 1–6). What attributes do you see in Daniel that you would like to emulate?

Women's Study

• Considering the cultural pressures our men must deal with, how can we as sisters in Christ be most helpful? How can we help men have character modeled after Jesus?

• What do you think we do that is harmful to our Christian brothers? What do we need to change?

Spend time in prayer for the men in your life.

Challenge

• Do or say something every day to build honor and respect into the lives of the men in your life.

Notes

_____

_____

_____

_____

_____

_____

_____

_____

_____

_____

_____

Notes

_____

_____

_____

_____

_____

_____

_____

_____

_____

_____

_____

Notes

_____

_____

_____

_____

_____

_____

_____

_____

_____

_____

_____

LESSON 6

Gut Check:

Committing to True Faith and Accountability

Introduction

Let's face it: Accountability is difficult. Accountability is a willingness to be held responsible for one's actions. It requires time, vulnerability, and honesty to be done right—all of which rely on discipline. It can be hard to find an accountability partner, hard to consistently meet with an accountability partner, hard to remain honest, and hard to offer advice without feeling like a hypocrite. Consequently, accountability is often something discussed but rarely practiced.

Men's Study

While we know the right thing to do, we don't always choose to do it. Having the guts to stand up for what we believe in requires courage. Think about soldiers. We hold them in high regard because they put their lives on the line for others. If a soldier put on the uniform but then ran away during battle, we would be disappointed. Upon seeing a soldier's uniform, people assume they are courageous, sacrificial, and loyal. Similarly, people should be able to tell what Christians stand for by the way we live our lives.

People will know that we believe in God when we have the courage to live differently. Some of those differences might be that we protect others instead of bullying them, are humble instead of arrogant, and respectfully cherish women instead of objectifying them. It also takes courage to form accountable relationships with other men. We shouldn't try to go it alone—we need to be vulnerable, admit failure, and accept help so we can stay on the right path.

In this lesson, we'll be challenged to be courageous in the following ways:

• Standing up for what we believe in

• Living differently

- Forming accountable relationships

- Admitting failure and accepting help

Which of these is hardest for you? Why?

Examine the stand Joshua makes in Joshua 24:15. He stands up for what he believes in despite opposition, maintains integrity, and has the courage to proclaim devotion to the Lord.

One way to maintain courage is through accountability partners. An accountability partnership is one in which two people are honest about their struggles and offer consistent encouragement to implement better spiritual habits and character.

- Do you have an accountability partner? Why or why not?

- Are you mentoring a younger man? Why or why not?

- What makes accountability difficult for you?

- What does an effective accountability partnership look like?

Read:

  ▫ Psalm 27:1

  ▫ Ecclesiastes 4:9–12

Doing what's right (and often, not popular) even when no one is watching takes real strength of character. Doing what's right requires a deep humility to look out for others rather than only for ourselves. It also takes genuine courage to pursue accountability, knowing that others can help us grow rather than going it alone. In God's eyes, a real man has the strength to submit to Him and to live with honor.

Challenge

- Find an accountability partner.

- Start mentoring a younger man.

- Help other men form accountable relationships.

Women's Study

Women's accountability partnerships have the potential to turn into gossip fests. True accountability involves genuine vulnerability, honesty, conviction, and encouragement. Accountability helps us to stand up for what we believe in, live differently, admit failure, and receive help. An accountability partnership is one in which two people are honest about their struggles and offer consistent encouragement to implement better spiritual habits and character.

- Do you have an accountability partner? Why or why not?

- Are you mentoring a younger woman? Why or why not?

- What makes accountability difficult for you?

- What does an effective accountability partnership look like?

Read and discuss Ecclesiastes 4:9–12.

Why do you think men struggle with accountability?

Women should be aware that men who decide to live according to Scripture may be considered weak, insignificant, and even feminine by our culture. Nevertheless, doing what's right (and often, not popular) even when no one is watching takes real strength of character. Doing what's right requires a deep humility to look out for others rather than only for ourselves. It also takes genuine courage for men to pursue accountability, knowing that others can help them grow rather than going it alone. In

God's eyes, a real man has the strength to submit to Him and to live with honor.

A lot of stuff that happens in church is more geared toward women than toward men. Singing, standing around holding hands, or sharing about personal lives makes many men feel uncomfortable. Churches should be more intentional to include activities that put men at ease. Men want to be active in their faith. How can we use that drive for the good of our church and the community?

- How can we encourage men to be a part of accountability partnerships?

- How can we encourage men's courageous spirit for adventure toward godly things?

Challenge

- Find an accountability partner.

- Start mentoring a younger woman.

- Help other women form accountability partnerships.

- Encourage men to have accountability partners.

Notes

Notes

LESSON 7

The Lost Art of Being a Gentleman:

Becoming Loving Husbands

Introduction

Unfortunately, in our culture, there is an increasing lack of appreciation for men who hold a door open for women or carry bags for them. In fact, some women may even respond harshly to such gestures, as if men are belittling them rather than trying to serve them.

As we've discussed, our culture has warped ways of defining masculinity and femininity. Over the last few decades, there has been a movement toward women exerting and being given more value, freedom, and opportunity. However, in other ways the movement has served to emasculate men.

What makes men feel emasculated?

Our culture emasculates men by making them feel less manly if they aren't tough, successful, or athletic. God created men with unique gifts, roles, and needs. It's important to understand what those are so we can best empower young men to become godly men.

Let's look at how God created the two genders to be different:

- Men tend to prefer things that are physical or mechanical. They like to be active and hands-on, figuring out how things work. They're kinesthetic and visual learners who connect with others by doing things together. Men are focused on facts, like to be problem solvers, and have a competitive nature. They feel a strong need to provide and protect.

- Men and women also differ in how they communicate. How many words do you think a man speaks on average in a day? (The answer is 3,000.) How many do you think a woman speaks on average in a day? (The answer is 20,000.) Men tend to communicate primarily using the left side of their brain for verbal reasoning, which means they tend to be more straightforward and logical. Women's brains are more functionally interconnected, which makes things like multitasking, reading emotions, and demonstrating intuition more natural for women.

- Women tend to be uniquely oriented toward people and how they feel. They connect verbally and are mostly verbal and auditory learners. Women like to discuss, are empathetic, have a strong need to connect, and tend to be more emotional.

Sometimes, instead of appreciating each other's differences, we allow ourselves to compare and devalue one another.

That's a very broad and basic look at how men and women differ, but they have at least one thing in common: Both men and women must deal with false messages from our culture that pull them away from what God wants them to be. For example, women struggle to feel beautiful because our culture focuses so much on the external. But God is concerned with what's on the inside. Men struggle to feel manly because our culture focuses so much on being macho and successful. But God wants them to be concerned with being courageous and hardworking. When we understand what each gender struggles with, we can better encourage one another.

Scripture lets us know how to encourage one another. From Ephesians 5:33, we saw that men are called to love women, and women are called to respect men. Remember, God designed us and knows what we need. Because He knows that a woman's greatest need is to feel loved, cherished, listened to, and cared for, He commands the man to do this fully. God also knows that a man's greatest need is to feel respected, valued, supported, and trusted, so He commands the woman to do this fully. The problem, though, is that our society makes women feel inferior and insignificant if they respect and honor men as leaders. This can make men feel unsure about leading or serving.

Men's Study

- What is the hardest thing about trying to be a godly man in our society?

- Men are called to humbly serve, love, and protect the women in their lives. What are some tangible ways you can do that?

- One day, you'll be a husband leading your own family. How do you want that to look?

- How can you grow now to become a better man of honor?

Close in prayer.

Challenge

Love and respect energize and empower people—it's the reason we're called to build one another up. Apply this lesson toward your dad, mom, siblings, and friends of the opposite gender, and hold on to these truths for your marriage someday.

Women's Study

- Women are called to humbly serve, respect, and support the men in their lives. What are some tangible ways you can do that?

- What are some things you need to change about your interactions with men?

- What do you want your husband and children's father to be like? How can you start to cultivate that now?

Close in prayer.

Challenge

Love and respect energize and empower people—that's the reason we're called to build one another up. Apply this lesson toward your dad, mom, siblings, and friends of the opposite sex, and hold on to these truths for your marriage someday.

Notes

_____

_____

_____

_____

_____

_____

_____

_____

_____

_____

Notes

_____

_____

_____

_____

_____

_____

_____

_____

_____

_____

_____

LESSON 8

Saying versus Doing:

Acting on Conviction

Introduction

Let's be honest. It would be greatly disappointing if we spent almost two months going through these lessons only to acknowledge some good ideas about how to live to honor God but not actually apply any of them. Don't get me wrong; there is value in good discussion of ideas. Sometimes, though, we talk too much. We discuss how we think God might want us to live instead of focusing on actually following through. Being a young person of conviction means hearing the truth and then acting on it. We don't just say something is the right thing to do—we live it.

If we're going to truly live as men of honor and women of worth, we're going to stand out from our culture—that's the whole point! It's what we're called to do so God can shine light into our dark world. If we compromise or back down, the darkness takes over the light. It's easy to get caught in bad cycles of thought and choices. We need to break the cycle, identify the lies from Satan and our culture, and stand firm on the foundation that we have the joy and strength of Christ when we live with honor and worth.

The difference in young people who are centered in God's love and grace is noticeable. Instead of living like a hamster on a wheel constantly chasing the fleeting pleasures of our culture, a godly young person stands confident in what he believes in, passionately pursues purpose, and joyfully serves others. Accept God's love for you as a gift and offer Him the best gift you can in return: Live as a man of honor or a woman of worth.

Too often, we want immediate results. We want to snap our fingers, say the perfect prayer, and become somebody totally different overnight. That's not how it happens. True discipleship is an everyday commitment. In this lesson, we're going to discuss key principles that will help you know who God is calling you to be and how to make choices that flesh out God's purpose in your life.

What does true discipleship look like? What defines a disciple of Christ?

• It's easy to have the wrong kind of discipline in our faith, adhering to a rigid schedule of religious practices but lacking authentic engagement. It's also easy to lack discipline and fail to meet with God at all because of laziness or excuses. Which of these tendencies are you prone to exhibit? Why?

Think about your relationships. What makes them meaningful and authentic? If we want our relationship with Christ to flourish, we have to spend time with Him, talk to Him, worship Him, and serve Him.

Why do we repeatedly come up with the same answers about how to strengthen our relationship with the Lord but fail to act on them?

Bible Study

In the Old Testament book of Exodus, we read about God choosing Moses to lead the Israelites out of slavery in Egypt. It's an incredible story of God's provision and faithfulness! You might imagine that the Israelites would demonstrate faithfulness in return, but only a few chapters into the narrative, we read about how they turn to other gods.

Read Exodus 32:1–4; 7–8.

God had blessed His people with gold when they left Egypt (Exod. 12:35–36), but the blessing was used wrongly by the sinful hearts of the people. Although God so powerfully delivered them from slavery, their faith in Him faded easily.

- Why do you think the Israelites asked Aaron to make them a god?

- Why was Aaron willing to go along with their request?

- What is your reaction to the Israelites making a false god?

We can cast judgment all we want about how ridiculous the Israelites acted, but the truth is, we make the same mistake all the time. We worship gods, not God. We prioritize things like technology and relationships. Social media isn't necessarily a terrible thing, but when we make time to flip through Instagram for two hours a day but can't find five minutes to pray, perhaps there's a problem.

- Have you ever made a decision at church or camp when you really felt the presence of the Lord only to return home and go right back to the sinful choice you promised to turn away from? Why do you think this happened?

- What gods do you worship? What distracts you from worshipping only God?

- How impatient do you become with God? Are you steadfast, or do you try to take over and solve things on your own?

I'm sure that it broke God's heart to see his people so easily turn away from Him and put their trust in a golden statue, but I'm also sure it angered Him greatly. We serve a mighty God who does not appreciate our games and deception. When we read further in Exodus 32, we see there was severe punishment for the sinful choice the people made. Being followers of God and disciples of Christ is something we need to take seriously.

We're not commanded to be perfect, but we're called to run this Christian life as if we're a well-trained athlete giving it all we have. The Holy Spirit is with us to guide us, and we have instructions in the Bible. Are we listening to the Holy Spirit and following Scripture's instructions?

Read 1 Kings 19:11–13.

- What are we meant to take away from this passage?

- How often do you spend time waiting and listening for the Holy Spirit to speak to you?

- How does the Holy Spirit speak to you?

Read 2 Timothy 3:16–17.

- What are we meant to take away from this passage?

- Are there parts of Scripture that you like to ignore? Why?

- Are you consistently reading Scripture so you know how to live your life to honor the Lord and others?

Our relationship with God requires discipline—it's that simple. It's a daily journey of devotion, sacrifice, humility, repentance, and rededication. When we read about the early believers and church, we see that being a Christ-follower consumed their entire lives. They were all-in and radical!

Read Colossians 3:1–3.

If our focus is on God, He will always be the determining factor in our choices, words, and actions. We need to decide what our life is all about. God commands our all, but we'll be so blessed to live according to His will.

Close in prayer.

Challenge

- Make your faith your own by developing spiritual disciplines. Start reading your Bible consistently. Pray. Journal. Serve. Worship. Replace giving in to sinful temptations with seeking accountability and acting according to God's call.

Notes

_____

_____

_____

_____

_____

_____

_____

_____

_____

_____

_____

Notes

Notes

LESSON 9

Sex Is Not the Problem:

Lust Is

Introduction

Too often, when young people hear about sex from a Christian perspective, it's negative. But God created sex! Sex is wonderful, but it's meant for a specific purpose and in a certain context. God designed sex to be a physically pleasing act that unifies a man and a woman in the committed context of marriage. Our culture, though, tells us something different:

- We should just go with our sexual urges.

- It's impossible to wait for marriage to have sex.

- Sex is simply a physical act, not an emotional one.

- Doing everything but intercourse is fine.

So, here's the truth: Sex is not the problem—lust is. So, what is lust?

Discuss these statements from Joshua Harris's book *Sex Is Not the Problem, (Lust Is)*:

- "Lust is a sexual desire minus honor and holiness."

- "Lust is an idolatrous and ultimately insatiable desire that rejects God's rule and seeks satisfaction apart from Him."[6]

Let's clarify what lust is and what it isn't. Discuss whether the following statements are true:

- It's lustful to be attracted to someone or notice that he or she is good-looking.

- It's lustful to have a strong desire to have sex.

- It's lustful to anticipate and be excited about having sex within marriage.

- It's lustful when a man or woman becomes turned on without any conscious decision to do so.

- It's lustful to experience sexual temptation.[7]

None of these situations are necessarily lustful. Harris makes these helpful distinctions:

> What could turn them into lust is how we respond to them. The crux of lust is how we act on the urges and desires of our sexual drive. Noticing an attractive person is not wrong but undressing that person with our eyes is. A sexual thought that pops into our mind isn't necessarily lust, but it can quickly become lust if it's entertained or dwelled on. An excitement for sex within marriage isn't sin, but it can be tainted by lust if it's not tempered with patience and restraint.

> If we fail to make these distinctions, our fight against lust will be greatly hampered. On the one hand, we can wind up excusing sinful thoughts and actions as "just how we're made or impossible to control," which isn't

true at all. On the other hand, we may end up being ashamed of our sex drive, which God never intended.[8]

Bible Study

Though the source of lust is our own evil desires, the one offended is God. When we choose lust, we're rejecting God. Instead of trusting what He says is best for us, we tend to choose what feels good in the moment.

Read 1 Thessalonians 4:7–8.

Because lust is defined as a constant desire for more, God provides an edict to live a holy life because lustful desires pull us away from God.

Read Ephesians 5:3.

- What does "any kind of impurity" in this passage mean to you? You should understand that this can include lustful thoughts, inappropriate joking, and so on. Women should understand that their lust for a boyfriend or for attention is just as much of an issue as the more commonly defined objects of lust with which men struggle.

- Some young Christians are interested in "how far is too far." Based on this verse, what is a better question to ask?

- When you hear "not even a hint of sexual impurity" in Ephesians 5:3, how does it make you feel?

God's standard of "not even a hint" quickly brings us to the end of our own ability and effort. Willpower won't work. Only the power of the cross can break the power of sin. Despair or thinking that we can change won't work either. Only the motive of grace—trust in the undeserved favor of God—can inspire us to pursue holiness free from fear and shame.

We sometimes try to hide our sexuality from God, but we should remember that God created us as sexual beings with sexual desires. We shouldn't experience misplaced shame over this. One way to deal with misplaced shame is to surrender your sexuality to the Lord. He has the power and wisdom to help us live out our sexuality as He designed it to be.

- What did you take away from this lesson?
- How do we help one another maintain an appreciation/ excitement for God's vision for our sexuality while also dealing with the constant pressure of lust?

Close in prayer.

Challenge

- Memorize Ephesians 5:3.

Notes

_____

_____

_____

_____

_____

_____

_____

_____

_____

_____

_____

Notes

_____

_____

_____

_____

_____

_____

_____

_____

_____

_____

_____

LESSON 10

Application Time:

Learning How to Deal with Lust

Introduction

We've talked about how young Christians can develop a tainted view of sex. Sex was designed by God and it's His plan that it be an act within the context of marriage. We've identified that lust is the true problem, and in this lesson, we'll talk about how to deal with lust.

- What are some of the consequences of impurity?

- What are some of the rewards of purity?

To deal with lust, we need to have the proper motivation: to honor God and our future spouse with our current sexual behavior. Without this perspective and the strength of Christ, we can easily get caught up in a moment of physical desire or emotional insecurity.

Discuss this idea: When God says no to something, it is because He is saying yes to something better.

We need to take seriously the idea of engaging in sex—and other sexual activity—only within the context of marriage. When a husband and wife have sex, it's a living picture of the spiritual reality of the marriage: two people melded into one. Anything outside of this is only a substitute for the intimacy God intended.

Bible Study

Read Hebrews 13:4.

As we've discussed, willpower is not the solution for battling lust. When our willpower fails, we're overcome with guilt and shame—feelings that can make us feel even farther away from God. We tend to feel particularly crummy when we've messed up in the area of sexual sin. All sin separates us from God, and we need His strength to overcome temptation and His grace to redeem us. Our relationship with God is the most important battle strategy when it comes to sexual sin. We must stay close to God's heart and put on our spiritual armor.

Have you ever talked honestly with God about your sexuality? Consider the following prayers from *Sex Is Not the Problem*:

> God, I know you created me to be a sexual creature with sexual desires. I don't ask that you remove my desire but that you help me please you in my thoughts and actions regarding sex.
>
> God, in this moment my whole body seems to be screaming for sexual satisfaction. Would you please quiet those desires right now? My body was made for you and for holiness—not for sexual sin. Help me glorify you with my body.
>
> God, you made me for true and lasting pleasure. Fill me with confidence that you have good things in store for me—something much better than what lust has to offer.[9]

- How would praying prayers like this be helpful? In what situations would prayers like this be helpful?

Accountability is also important. What forms of accountability in regard to sexual temptation are most helpful for you?

Men and women are different because we were made to complement each other. We can either commit to sexual purity together and help one another or cause each other to stumble. Discuss the following statements:

- Men's sexual desire is often more physical; women's desire is more often rooted in emotional longings.

- Men are generally wired to be the sexual initiator and are stimulated visually; women are generally wired to be the sexual responder and are stimulated by touch.

- Men are created to pursue and even find the pursuit stimulating; women are made to want to be pursued and even find being pursued stimulating.

If these three statements are true, how can we be purposeful to help each other (the opposite gender) in our battle for purity?

Isn't it wonderful how God made men and women to interact with each other? But Satan takes what is good and twists it. Lust blurs true masculinity and femininity in harmful ways. For example, a young woman might believe she's unattractive because she's not being pursued and will therefore flirt or dress immodestly to get a man's attention. A young man might forget about a woman's heart, mind, and soul in his quest for physical pleasure.

- What are some of the lies that Satan uses to blur how we see/appreciate the opposite gender?

- What did you take away from this lesson?

- Remember that Ephesians 5:3 challenged us to have "not even a hint" of sexual impurity. What changes do you need to make so that, through God's strength, you have control over lust rather than lust having control over you?

Challenge

- Set up accountability specifically to address sexual temptation and sin. This could mean finding an accountability partner, putting protective software on your devices, or choosing to only watch movies in a public space.

Notes

Notes

LESSON 11

Building Beautiful Marriages:

Seeing the Joy of Intimacy as the Reward of Commitment

Introduction

The Bible has plenty to say about enjoying sex within the context of marriage, but Scripture doesn't necessarily lay out any ground rules about dating. So how should men of honor and women of worth approach dating? Well, let's talk about that.

Consider the following questions:

- What is the purpose of dating?

- When is it OK to date?

- What are appropriate sexual boundaries within a dating relationship?

We may not come to complete agreement on this topic, and that's OK, but I want you to consider this perspective:

> I'll wait until I'm ready for true commitment as a way of letting Christ's love control my relationships with the opposite gender. I'll stop seeing the opposite gender as potential boyfriends/girlfriends and start treating them as sisters/brothers in Christ. I'll stop worrying about having a boyfriend/girlfriend or getting married and trust God's timing. I'll stop flirting with temptation and instead focus on becoming a mature and godly man or woman. I'll be proud to give my future spouse the gift of my purity.

Discuss the ideas from this perspective:

- Do you have insecurities when you aren't in a relationship?

- Do you struggle with flirting?

- Do you think there is potential pain for your future spouse when you choose to date? Why or why not?

Bible Study

Read 2 Corinthians 6:14.

The Bible makes it clear that if we choose to date, we need to be in a relationship with someone who loves Jesus and demonstrates a maturing faith. Together, you can establish a relationship of mutual respect for the Lord and each other. As men of honor and women of worth, a dating relationship should be centered on a shared love for God and desire to honor Him.

God made the fulfillment of intimacy a by-product of commitment-based love. If we want to experience the goodness of His plan, we need to reconnect the pursuit of intimacy with the pursuit of commitment. In other words, dating should be done in a way that protects God's context for sexual connection.

Consider the following statement from *I Kissed Dating Goodbye*: "The joy of intimacy is the reward of commitment."[10]

- Do you agree? Why or why not?

- How does God define commitment? How does our culture define commitment?

- How do you think God would want you to go about dating?

- How can you date with your future spouse in mind?

- What did you take away from this lesson?

Challenge

- Come up with a personal dating plan. Determine when you will start dating, qualities you want your future spouse to have, and sexual boundaries you will establish with a boyfriend or girlfriend.

- Make a commitment to God that you will wait to enjoy sexual intimacy in marriage.

Notes

Notes

_____

_____

_____

_____

_____

_____

_____

_____

_____

_____

_____

_____

Notes

_____

_____

_____

_____

_____

_____

_____

_____

_____

_____

_____

ACKNOWLEDGMENTS

Many of the ideas fleshed out in this curriculum were originally dreamed up by a team of youth coaches at Vail Christian Church in Tucson, Arizona. To every person at that youth coach retreat, I say thank you, and I hope you are encouraged to know that many others may be blessed by what God laid on our hearts that day.

I currently serve at such a wonderful church with an amazing team: Trinity Church of Mesa. I value the staff's leadership and hearts to serve and the support of my church family.

NOTES

1. Kate Fox, "Mirror, Mirror: A Summary of Research Findings on Body Image," *Social Issues Research Centre* (1997), http://www.sirc.org/publik/mirror.html.

2. Ibid.

3. Robert S. McGee, *The Search for Significance: Seeing Your True Worth Through God's Eyes* (Nashville, TN: Thomas Nelson, 1984), 15.

4. Ginny Olson, *Teenage Girls: Exploring Issues Adolescent Girls Face and Strategies to Help Them* (Grand Rapids, MI: Zondervan, 2006), 101.

5. Steven Gerali, *Teenage Guys: Exploring Issues Adolescent Guys Face and Strategies to Help Them* (Grand Rapids, MI: Zondervan, 2006), 32–45.

6. Joshua Harris, *Sex Is Not the Problem, (Lust Is): Sexual Purity in a Lust-Saturated World* (Sisters, OR: Multnomah Books, 2008), 38.

7. Ibid, 35.

8. Ibid, 35–36.

9. Ibid, 37.

10. Joshua Harris, *I Kissed Dating Goodbye* (Sisters, OR: Multnomah Books, 1997), 28.

CPSIA information can be obtained
at www.ICGtesting.com
Printed in the USA
BVHW061331290621
610728BV00001B/195

9 781953 300478